Your **footprints** at age _____ Date _____

Left          Right

10 9 8 7 6 5 4 3 2 1

Printed in Hong Kong

Distributed in Canada by
Raincoast Books
8680 Cambie Street
Vancouver, B.C. V6P 6M9

Chronicle Books
85 Second Street
San Francisco, CA 94105
www.chroniclebooks.com/wegman

Photographs: William Wegman
Design: Empire Design Studio, nyc
Typeset in Interstate and Sabon

Lower right-hand image on the "Visitors" page: Painted photo backdrop
from the exhibition *From the Background to the Foreground: the Photo
Backdrop and Cultural Expression*, Visual Studies Workshop, from the
collection of Vasant Nayak. Upper left-hand image on the "Visitors" page:
Painted backdrop courtesy Mark Hunt.

ISBN: 0-8118-2392-X

# Baby Book

William Wegman

CHRONICLE BOOKS

# This book **belongs** to…

_Little James Witz_
_October 4th, 1999_

*The* _____ *Family*

*Father* _____

Birthplace _____ Date _____

Grandmother _____ | Grandfather _____

Birthplace _____ | Birthplace _____
Date _____ | Date _____

Great-Grandfather _____ | Great-Grandfather _____

Birthplace _____ | Birthplace _____
Date _____ | Date _____

Great-Grandmother _____ | Great-Grandmother _____

Birthplace _____ | Birthplace _____
Date _____ | Date _____

# Your Family Tree

*Mother*

Birthplace _____ Date _____

*Grandmother* _____ | *Grandfather* _____

Birthplace _____ | Birthplace _____
Date _____ | Date _____

*Great-Grandfather* _____ | *Great-Grandfather* _____

Birthplace _____ | Birthplace _____
Date _____ | Date _____

*Great-Grandmother* _____ | *Great-Grandmother* _____

Birthplace _____ | Birthplace _____
Date _____ | Date _____

# The Folks

Dad

Mom

Your **Mom** and **Dad**

Photograph

Photograph

Dad

Mom

How we met _through friends_

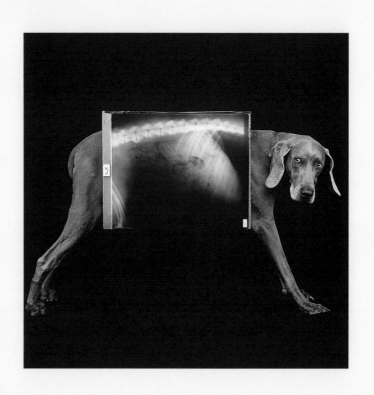

Baby **Belly** Picture

Did we know whether you were going to be a boy or a girl? *yes we did*

And did we tell anyone? *yes we did!*

_____ Date _____

Hot fudge, butterscotch and kiwis…unusual foods Mom craved while carrying you

tacos, mexican food, pasta

How Mom felt excited, happy

# Choosing your Name

Inspiration for your name  *Pete was from Grandfather Doty*
*James was from Papa Jones*

Names we liked

# Baby Shower

Gift _____ From _____ _____

Gift _____ From _____ _____

Gift _____ From _____ _____

Gift _____ From _____ _____

Gift _____ From _____ _____

Gift _____ From _____ _____

Gift _____ From _____ _____

Gift _____ From _____ _____

Gift _____ From _____ _____

Gift _____ From _____ _____

Gift _____ From _____ _____

Gift _____ From _____ _____

Gift _____ From _____ _____

Gift _____ From _____ _____

Gift _____ From _____ _____

# The Day you were Born

Place, Date and Time  Athens Regional Hospital - Athens, GA
10/4/99   4:10 AM

Your Weight  7 lbs 8 oz          Your Length  20 inches

                                          mom says / dad says
Hair Color  light brown          Eye Color  Steel gray / blue

Delivered by  Dr. Kelley

Other Attendees  Daddy, NaNa


Our Feelings  Tired! Exhilerated, Very Happy, nervous
Proud

# Wishes for You

Our wishes and hopes We want you to be happy, whatever
that means (especially if it means:
You go to HARVARD)*
You make sure to fulfill your ambitions & dreams
You make sure you are always your own person, and
never worry about what anyone else says (except
your Dad)

* JULIARD) IF YOU Become a musician, which would
also be great. Maybe you can go there for your
Doctorate

# Mother and Child

Photograph

Date and age

The Day you came Home

Home Sweet Home

What we felt

Date

# Family Portrait

And baby makes...

Date and age _____

# Visitors

Who they were and what they said  Mama
Papa
Aunt Barbara
Edward
Mik & May
Rich
Jen & Kathy

# You Roll Over, Crawl and Sit Up

Date and age

# Your First Steps

Date and age 12-16-00  14½ months old

Your First **Words**

What you said Daddy
Mama
Nana
Deer > Sight
Look
Dog
Duck

Other memorable sayings and actions

# Sleeping

The first time you slept through the night _____

_____

_____

_____ Date _____

How we helped you go to sleep _____

_____

_____

_____

When you first recognized Mom and Dad _____

_____

_____

_____

_____ Date _____

# First Tooth

Your first **tooth** appeared on _____

_____

_____


Your first **smile** was on _____

_____

_____


You first ate **solid food** on _____

_____

_____


You first **used a spoon** on _____

_____

_____

# A Lock of your Hair

Date and age _____

# First Bath

Splash!

Date and age

# First Outing

Ticket to Ride

Date and destination

# First Mischief

The date and the deed

Other trouble you got into

# First Friends

Name(s) and date _____

_____

_____

# Animal Friends

Photograph

Name(s) and date

# Favorite Toy

Your favorite **toy**

Your favorite **song**

Your favorite **video**

Your favorite **game**

Boo!

You dressed up as _____

_____

_____

First Holiday Season

Season's Greetings

How we celebrated with you _____

_____

_____

# First Birthday

Happy Birthday!

Who came to your party